HOW TO BECOME A PILOT IN EUROPE:

COMPLETE PILOT TRAINING GUIDE

Kudzanai Chikohora

Kudzanai Chikohora

How To Become A Pilot in Europe:
Complete Pilot Training Guide

ISBN: 979-86-6678-200-2

CONTENTS

CHAPTER 1: INTRODUCTION

Thank you for choosing this book, or more accurately, guide. I decided to write it to provide honest advice about how you can become a commercial pilot without remortgaging your parents' house or getting a £100k plus loan financed at 4% above the base rate - basically getting screwed over financially for the rest of your life! I did a quick search of Google on 'how to become a pilot' and I can't say I was impressed with the results. The first offering was from the UK University Admissions website. They reference an integrated training provider that is effectively the most expensive flight training a student could find, with most students having to self-finance and without any guarantee of a job on successful completion. I'll give the university website the benefit of the doubt as I suspect the article was written by a careers officer who does not have any flying experience, but merely trying to do their best juggling many other tasks in his or her inbox with the powers of Google. The next result was from the UK flag carrier. Google has decided to rank these high on the flight training subject. Cheap flight to Europe? Perhaps, but I'm not sure if I would go there for flight training advice though. They do have a pretty significant marketing department and budget – so it is making more sense now why they get so high on Google. Can you tell that I am reading a book on Search Engine Optimisation at the moment to raise the profile of my blog on Google? (If you are interested in doing this yourself, read Tim Kitchen's 'How to get to the top of Google' - you won't be disappointed). Also, as a thank you for buying this book, you can subscribe to kcthepilot.com for free updates.

Away from the Search Engine Optimisation and back to flight training. The top search results are all advertising from the most expensive flight training schools, which the majority of prospective pilots won't be able to afford.

Instead, the flying school will suggest you remortgage your parents' house to fund your training, and you will be encouraged to sign a training contract that says pay us £100k plus and we will try our best to get you a job, but if we don't, unlucky, that's your problem! If you want a guide with genuine honesty about the alternatives available to you on how you can become a pilot through a combination hard work, common sense and yes, of course, money, please read on.

I was lucky and got to the right-hand seat of a 70-tonne jet juggling a full-time job and also did it in a record 12 months at a fraction of what it cost others. I am not particularly gifted in any way, but worked hard and tried to be efficient with time and money. WARNING- FLIGHT TRAINING IS BLOODY EXPENSIVE and EMOTIONALLY DRAINING, so let's not make the process any more expensive or painful than it needs to be.

I somehow managed to get a Master's Degree in Aerospace Engineering from the University of Manchester back in 2008. I was a chartered engineer in the oil and gas industry for just over 11 years before switching to flying professionally. I was okay as a student. The one thing that I managed to remember from uni, was that before writing any papers, and later technical documents, you had to 'scope out'; or if you prefer, ring-fence the limits of your work. i.e. make all your excuses up front! I have tried to be concise and focus on the areas that will make a difference to your success in flight training and highlight ways to save you time and money during pilot training. If I don't know enough about a given subject to pass comment or judgment, I have generally said so and left it out e.g. Upset Recovery and Awareness Training in an aircraft. This was not a requirement as I went through training.

This guide is based on the European (EASA) system of flight training. My experience is modular flight training, i.e. pay as you go in stages as you would for a DIY house renovation. You may work through one room at a time over many months or even years until completion. However, unlike DIY renovation, certain stages have to be completed within a specific timeframe. So, it's advisable to think through the process carefully and plan. Welcome to modular flight training.

I will first talk about integrated courses. Unlike modular courses, where you complete it in chunks, sometimes with different training providers, integrated courses are based on having all the training under one organisation for a set price. There is no mention of modular courses on the top google searches on how to become a pilot. Yet, the Modular avenue is probably the cheapest way of doing flight training for most. I will share all I can about how to keep costs down, but flight training is still costly. You will need £50-70k depending on your efforts for risk vs reward vs time put into researching/willingness to disrupt your way of life.

My standard of English writing is not first-class, nor am I a professional editor. I'm sure that you would prefer that I put things across as plainly and as concise as possible. You will hopefully forgive my spelling, grammar and punctuation. My very kind family and friends who are much more capable than I have read and edited this guide, but I suspect there will be only so much they can salvage.

CHAPTER 2: START EARLY AND MAKE USE OF FLYING SCHOLARSHIPS

"I'm 35 years old, am I too old to start flight training and will I be able to get a job'? This question continues to appear on the various forums. The answer is, the outcome of your training is the critical factor and whether or not you get through is in your hands. If you think that you are too old and the airlines will discriminate against you for a younger model for first right-hand seat opportunity, then that will be the outcome! The forums are riddled with keyboard warriors that have a score to settle. The bottom line, from my experience, is that the airlines don't particularly care (within reason) how old you are. The first time I flew the 737 was just before my 34th birthday and it was around 18 months prior that I started my modular pilot training. The airlines are primarily interested in your ability to satisfy the 8 International Civil Aviation Authority (ICAO) pilot competencies. I mention these now not to send you to sleep but to give you the basics of how the airline world works in how flight crews are assessed. The competencies are: Communication, Aircraft Flight Path Management (Manual Control), Aircraft Flight Path Management (Automation), Leadership and Teamwork, Problem Solving and Decision Making, Application of procedures, Workload Management and Situational Awareness.

Some of these competencies are developed during your flight training, but a significant amount is studied away from the flight deck. My 11 years in the oil and gas industry without a shadow of doubt helped me develop some of the softer competencies communication, leadership and teamwork and in workload management. I remain convinced that the version of me at 21 years of age would have been a total nightmare to spend time within the flight deck. I was sure at that age I knew everything and it took me a solid ten years later to figure out the truth was the complete opposite. The older you are and the more experience you have makes you more resilient as you meet some of lifes' challenges, in particular overcoming failure. That said, a 21-year-old may not have the life experience, but they do have other advantages. They tend to be able to learn much quicker and absorb information much faster. Their hand-eye coordination and reactions are quicker too. Developing some of the 'non-core' flying competencies such as teamwork and problem solving through extracurricular activities at school and university (clubs, societies, sports) and part-time jobs etc., can facilitate achieving the grade. Age is not critical - ability is. During interviews, the airlines are trying to determine if the candidate is a training risk and how would I feel if I had to sit next to this person for 12 hours in the confined space of a flight deck? The goal is to be able to answer those two questions successfully when your opportunity comes.

So why did I start this section focusing on the end product? One of the things that helped drive my training and stay motivated during the difficult patches (there will be many) and eventually land the airline job, was to keep the end goal in sight and keep referring back to it. Right from the start, I was around professional pilots - gliding is excellent for this. I was able to ask them many questions along the way and observe the performance standards I had to achieve to reach my goal. I would recommend to the reader currently thinking about or is currently undergoing flight training, be that via the modular or integrated route.

While acknowledging age is not a critical factor, I would advise you to start flying as young as possible if you can! The reason I say this is that the earlier you can begin your flight training, the sooner that education knowledge starts accumulating and in turn grows and compounds over the years. It is a bit like investing and compound interest. If you love aviation, this should be easy and enjoyable. I get messages all the time with people complaining that they don't have money to make a start on flight training, but they want to. There are many things you can do, which are outside the formal flight training structure that cost relatively little, but can get you started and can make a difference. Watch YouTube videos, play flight simulator, go to your local airfield, go to air shows, get absorbed in it all. It all eventually adds up and may one day make the difference for you when you are sat in front of an assessor and trying to find common ground.

My real flying education started in my first or second year of secondary school. We were lucky enough to have 'aero club' once a week and would either build model aeroplanes or watch aviation videos. The first one was a flight deck video of a Cathay Pacific Boeing 747-400 from Heathrow to the old airport in Hong Kong (Kai Tak) with the infamous chequered board approach. At 13 years old I had Assumed Temperature, and Thrust De-rating explained to me, including how take-off thrust is set. Twenty years later I would be on my type rating on the 737 and not have any issues. Absorb all the information you can find.

The next key point about the advantages of starting early is that you have many more avenues to obtain free-flying and participate in flying scholarships. I joined the air cadets and each year we would have one or two air experience flights lasting 20 minutes to an hour. By the time I commenced my Private Pilot Licence (PPL), I had logged 2.5 hours purely from cadet air experience flights. To the young reader, find your local air cadets and get involved. Aside from flying, Air Cadets provide many opportunities to learn and develop some of the ICAO competencies described above during many of the adventure camps you will participate in: communication, leadership and teamwork, problem-solving and decision making. These competencies will not suddenly 'appear' in the week before your airline assessment or during the two hours simulator prep you have booked a day or two before your airline assessment. Simulator prep is a brush-up session to practice various manoeuvres just before you go for an airline assessment. In a way, you determine the outcome of your airline assessment many years before you even apply for the job. What work are you doing today to improve your chances of passing an airline assessment and a type rating in maybe 5, 10 or in my case 20 years' time? It was not apparent at all to me that would be the case, but I got involved. The sum of your life experiences from a very early age can contribute to opportunities for securing employment many years down the line.

When you are in your mid-teens the air cadet organisation will have gliding scholarships available. I applied and got one of these. The prerequisite was that you had to have completed a gliding introductory course which is open every so often through your local air cadet branch. During my gliding scholarship, most of the instructors were active fast-jet Royal Air Force pilots or professional pilots in one way or another. As I touched on earlier, the head start it gives you to just be around these types of people; standards, work ethic, etc., will help you. It also feeds the dream as you begin to realise that people flying fast military jets, or a skipper on a jumbo jet are not superhumans; they are regular people just like you. If you do well during your gliding scholarship, there is a further route available to complete the advanced glider training course and subsequently, train to become a gliding instructor. This is all completely FREE. Gliding helped me so much – both at school and later at university when I could not afford to pay £150/hr for powered flying training. In air cadet gliding, before you were sent solo (conducting a flight on your own without an instructor), you had to fly with a senior instructor (usually the chief flying instructor or their deputy). The earlier you get used to 'flight check rides' - a flying exam, the more comfortable life is later on during high stakes flying test or checks. They do not go away, and the pressure does not get any easier.

Towards the end of my time in the cadets I was awarded a powered flying scholarship. The powered flying scholarship was 12 hours in a single-engine aircraft aimed at achieving solo standard. I did mine with Tayside Aviation in Dundee. With all the gliding experience I had under my belt, I was ready and able to go solo after just 6 hours on the course. The rest of the time was spent consolidating. Get involved if you can by finding your air cadet organisation and locating your local station. I have already mentioned modular vs integrated flight training, but the military path is often completely overlooked. Military flying is another route for the reader, and again, the earlier you start the more chance you give yourself to pass military pilot selection. A background in the cadets will provide you with an excellent basis to convince the selection board that you have what it takes.

The Air League is another terrific organisation that has flying scholarships. The Air League is an aviation and aerospace charity focused on changing lives through aviation. Finally, I wanted to mention the Honourable Company of Air Pilots. The Honourable Company of Air Pilots are focused on sponsoring and encouraging aviation activities. I was awarded a PPL scholarship towards the end of my time in university. I would encourage the reader to look into these opportunities if you fit the criteria. The key to winning these scholarships is to recognise that it is not a one-way relationship. You have to be able to demonstrate that you have given back or will do so in one way or another. A glance of the Honourable Company of Air Pilot

Scholarship winners for 2019, shows out of the ten PPL scholarships, five went to existing glider pilots or candidates that had already been in the air cadets/won other awards. In the air cadets, I ran the cadet section at my school for several years, and that brought many learnings and experiences. This allowed me to get to the top of the candidate selection as typically many of these applications and interviews rely on passing some sort of competency-based interview or someone else putting you forward. You will not be put forward if you do nothing outside of the norm. If you look at all the scholarship winners who are successful in the Honourable Company of Air Pilot Scholarships, most of them have made some contribution to help others, and it may not necessarily be within the flying context.

For me, during university, I formed and ran the university gliding society. I wanted to fly at university even after I was no longer eligible for the university air squadron (immigration rules to being aircrew in the RAF had changed). My role in the gliding society included organising funding, finding a good base, obtain all the resources to allow us to set up a successful club and compete amongst other the university gliding clubs around the country. We were ranked 3rd nationally; a remarkable achievement for us all at the university of Manchester gliding club given we had only formed two years prior. Of course, I did not do it on my own. We had an incredible committee, and without teamwork, none of it would have been possible. I mentioned my university gliding experience because that was a really important step in allowing me to continue flying at very low cost when I had very little money. This may be something you wish to consider if you are going to university.

The interview panel for my PPL scholarship was with two senior retired RAF officers and at the time the 777-fleet manager for a national carrier. My cadet experience allowed me to spoke the 'language' of the RAF officers. A few years prior, I had borrowed from my local library and read '21st Century Jet – the making of the Boeing 777'. I had no idea the significance that the book would have on the outcome of my life when I read it just out of natural curiosity. I knew there were eight scholarships up for grabs. Being shortlisted for interview, I briefed myself that I did not have to be the 'best' candidate, but I just had to make it difficult for the interview panel to send me home empty-handed. Thankfully, I did make it difficult for them to send me home and a few days later I received the phone call with the good news. The message for the reader is: if I had not gone to aero club, then air cadets, then gliding scholarship, then flying scholarship, then getting turned down by the University Air Squadron, subsequently leading to forming and running a gliding society, I would have just been another name in the PPL scholarship application pile. I would never have been invited for interview and had the opportunity to make the connection with the officers from my cadet experiences and talk shop with the Boing 777 fleet manager.

Start the learning process early with the resources you have available – it doesn't particularly matter if you don't have £8k to spend on a PPL immediately or £120k to spend on an integrated course. Just immerse yourself with what you have and eventually an opportunity will present itself to help you progress.

Chapter 3: First flight and medical

Assuming you have not had a flying lesson before, the first step is to book a trial or taster flight for 30 mins or an hour to see if flying is for you. The trial flight is an excellent way to get going without committing vast sums of money. To book your trial flight I advise you to shop around. I have typically found the smaller the airfield and the flying school, the lower the costs. I would also recommend that you book directly with your chosen flying school (Google should yield good results). Avoid booking via 'adventure day' websites, for example, those selling hot air balloon flights, race track experiences etc. While the trial flight is just a taster, it allows you to research and get a feel for what your PPL 'experience' will be like. This will also be an opportunity to review your prospective flying school.

The next section covers what I would consider flight school selection criteria:

Which airfield?

- When choosing where to do your flight training, particularly for PPL, I would say stay away from international airports. Although mixing with the jets can seem exciting, you want to spend your money on actual pilot training. Larger airports prioritise commercial traffic which can lead to PPL students having to 'hold' - aviation speak for being sent to the waiting room during your lessons because you need to get out of the way of a commercial jet that is about to land or take off. You will still be charged per hour for flight training irrespective of your lesson being paused because you had to orbit for 10-15 mins because of incoming jet traffic.

- An international airport is typically a more complex airfield. This translates to a slightly longer duration PPL (which is more expensive for you) as it takes just that much longer to grasp some of the additional procedural requirements.
- The weather tends to be worse at higher elevation airfields. Pick lower elevation airfields if the option allows
- One further consideration you need to make is the actual surface of the airfield. If flying from a grass strip, you may find the airport becomes waterlogged and frozen in the winter, causing it to close for some time. Again, this will slow your training down.

The user will find they have to assess all the variables and come up with a solution that works best for them. From the above, it should be clear that there is no such thing as a perfect flying school. All have their advantages and disadvantages. The key is to find a school that works for you and your particular situation for the majority of the time. It will not always be perfect.

Instructor availability is essential

- You do not want to commit to a PPL course and find that after your first five lessons, there is no longer instructor coverage during the weekends, for example.
- Lack of weekend instructor coverage would be extreme and unusual, but you need to figure out when you will be flying and make sure that there will be an instructor available on those days.
- Other customer service considerations include

how responsive the flying school is? Do they return your calls straight away or are you leaving voicemail after voicemail with no callback? Some flying schools may not necessarily have a front desk and rely on instructors returning calls between lessons. Okay if someone is getting back to you, but if you find no one is responding, this is probably a good sign that you need to look elsewhere.

- After your trial flight, you will hopefully want to meet and have a discussion with your instructor, particularly if you are committing to an £8k-10k PPL course.

How many different instructors will teach you?

- While flying schools need to manage their resources as best they can, it is crucial for you as a paying customer to have consistency of instruction. Imagine that when you were learning to drive, you had a new instructor for each lesson. What would this do to your progress? You need to apply the same thinking for flight instruction. During my PPL I had one primary instructor who took me for the majority of lessons and occasionally if they were not available, someone else would cover.

- Flight training can be challenging and instructors will be reluctant to allow you to do certain things, particularly if they have not flown with you previously. Your student notes will go some way to brief a given instructor on your progress, but it is much more efficient if you can keep the same instructor for as much of the course as possible; as they start to learn what you are like and can optimise the instruction to suit.

- When you attempt to book your trial flight or

lesson, what is the availability of flying slots? The excellent schools tend to be reasonably busy and in my experience, to get all the flying slots I wanted, I needed to book around 4 - 6 weeks in advance as soon as the calendar was open. The reader will need to apply some common sense. If the school seems reputable and has had good reviews, then it may make sense to 'wait' until slots become available for your PPL. If on the other hand there is no availability for several months, then go somewhere else.

An excellent resource of information on PPL training, including specific flying schools, are Facebook groups. Find one and ask for feedback or advice if you are not sure. I have shared a link to one of the Facebook groups on my blog available at kcthepilot.com/book. The information on Facebook groups can be handy. Do use it with caution though as unfortunately, there is no fact-checking or real moderation. If a person has an isolated negative viewpoint on a given flight school, consider it but do not write that institution off completely. If on the other hand, 5 or 10 people are consistently saying the same thing about a school (good or bad) it is likely to be accurate.

Once you have selected your flight school and booked out a trial lesson, we are ready to go flying! There is no requirement to bring anything with you to the trial flight experience other than some sort of ID and perhaps your wallet! There will be a form to fill out with for your personal details and next of kin information. If you have any underlying health conditions that you think may impact your ability to take part in the trial lesson, please discuss this with the flight school and seek medical advice beforehand. You do not need to complete a flying medical before your trial flight at this point - we are still at the 'is flying for me' stage. Apply common sense to your lesson. Get a good night's sleep beforehand, no alcohol etc. and enjoy yourself on the day.

Once airborne, you may have the opportunity to manipulate the controls under the instructors' supervision. Do as much or as little as you feel comfortable with provided the instructor is happy. After the flight ensure you obtain your certificate verifying that you have had 30 mins or 1 hour in the aircraft even though you may still be undecided about continuing your flying journey. This trial flight hour counts towards your total hours for licensing purposes, so do not let it go to waste by not having it recorded. The usual way to record this hour would be to start a flying logbook. Your flying school will show you how to obtain a log and how to keep it up to date. If you have decided that you want to pursue flying, then excellent, buy a logbook.

Your medical

This part can often cause a lot of anguish, but it needn't had. I am not a medical officer so I will not discuss in detail the technicalities of what is required and what testing will take place. What I can share is advice on how to get through and the minimum level of medical necessary for the least expense to the reader.

As I mentioned at the start of this guide, I will only be focusing on the 'full PPL', which is the European Union Aviation Safety Agency (EASA) PPL. EASA set the rules for aviation in Europe. Our local authority in the UK, the Civil Aviation Authority (CAA) is responsible for implementing those standards. The minimum level of medical required for PPL is a Class 2 medical. The minimum level of medical needed to fly commercially (after PPL) is a class 1. There are other versions of the PPL specific to the UK that do not require you to have a CAA class 1 or class

2 medical. They are not in the scope of this guide as I assume the reader will be approaching their flight training based on potentially building on their PPL to achieve various professional flight training qualifications. The other versions of the PPL do not allow you to develop and add to it.

If you have no commercial ambitions (for now anyway), a Class 2 medical will suffice. Compared to the Class 1 medical, the class 2 medical is cheaper and is not as stringent, for example, the time between assessments etc. The advantage of a Class 2 medical is you can have the assessments carried out much more readily by an Aero Medical Examiner (AME) - a doctor who is authorised and qualified to check your fitness to be a pilot.

The Class 1 medical is a requirement to fly professionally. If you want to fly professionally, you need to know if there is any medical reason which would preclude you from doing so. Class 1 medicals can only be completed at a few specific centres and you can find an AME on the CAA website. At the time of writing, a Class 1 medical cost around £600. A Class 2 medical is about 30-40% less. A Class 1 medical is typically renewed annually (with the associated expense) although that interval can be shortened due to age or underlying conditions. A Class 2 medical is more generous with renewal intervals, but still is driven by your age, health and any underlying health conditions.

Most people do not realise that a good number of medicals are not issued on the same day that the assessment takes place. This is something you need to consider. In my case, it took around four months for my initial Class 1 medical to be issued from my first appointment. If there are any question marks during your examination that need to be followed up with additional documentation from your doctor, then this takes time. Quite routinely, further tests may be necessary if the AME is not satisfied that you meet the CAA requirements for a particular area. This is not necessarily a permanent rejection and that you are not able to meet the Class 1 requirements; it could be that further tests or information are required. For those in the UK, if an issue is found during your medical and you need to be referred to a specialist, one of the things that worked well for me was that I had private medical insurance at the time. I went to my GP, advised what the issue was and obtained a referral to go private. The problem for me was an anomaly with my blood pressure requiring me to be monitored over 24 hours. I had the monitoring undertaken, and the report submitted to my AME. The results showed there was nothing amiss, and my Class 1 medical was subsequently issued. All this takes time, so do not leave your medical examination to the last minute if at all possible.

I initially had a Class 2 medical assessment when I was doing my PPL. While I hoped to fly commercially, I knew this would not be immediate, so I settled for a lower cost and more accessible Class 2 medical before upgrading later.

There are steps that you can take to prepare for your medical: If you have underlying conditions, it is worth bringing them to the attention of the AME when you book your medical before your appointment. They may request additional documentation before your meeting and this will save you time in the long run. If you have not had your eyes tested in a while (most people don't), many opticians offer free eye tests. Get your eyes tested before your Class 1 or Class 2 appointment. Similarly, if your ears are like mine and tend to have wax build-up, visit your GP to have them checked and if necessary, cleaned before your examination. Avoid heavy drinking in the days before your medical. Be well rested and try to eat normally avoiding too much coffee and energy drinks just before your medical.

The final part is, don't worry. The medical can be stressful, but try to relax. Ultimately, the AME wants to issue you with your medical, so try to make that task as easy for them as possible by doing what you can to prepare beforehand and taking a common-sense approach in looking after your body. If you fail your medical, not all hope is lost. The AME will explain why and advise what the next steps would be. If unfortunately, a medical reason precludes you from passing a Class 1 or Class 2 medical, and you still have a burning desire to fly, then it may be worth investigating other flying options that do not require you to have a Class 1 or Class 2 medical such as the National Private Pilots Licence.

CHAPTER 4: MODULAR VS INTEGRATED COURSES

With the medical complete, your next step is to decide which training route to follow. There are two routes available to complete your pilot training. You don't necessarily have to wait until you have a medical, but can start doing your research beforehand.

Integrated courses

The first type of course is an integrated course. An integrated course is an all-in-one package that is based on a student starting without any flying experience and finishing in around 18 months with what is known as a frozen Air Transport Pilots Licence (fATPL). The school provides all aspects of training for an all-inclusive price. Integrated courses will typically, for the larger mainstream schools, have some kind of admission and screening process ahead of the course with the student having to pay for the screening. However, there are exceptions where the student is not required to fund their selection.

A few schools provide some kind of performance guarantee, i.e. if you fail a given part of the training, the extra remedial work will be carried out free of charge. Exceptionally if the student is still unable to pass the course, they can expect an element of course fees to be refunded.

Some integrated courses have the advantage of providing students with the option to apply to an airline before they start their training. If successful in the application, the student is provided with a conditional offer of employment. One such condition will be that the student completes all training to a given standard. At the end of the training, the student will commence employment with the partner airline subject to a position still being available. These students are referred to as 'tagged' when going through their flight training. There may be a requirement to complete a streamlined/fast track interview with the airline. The airline interview panel will typically include an HR and pilot representative. There may be a simulator check ride too. In any case, the student is prioritised for employment.

Integrated tagged schemes are great when the airline industry is doing well but, most recently during COVID-19 crisis, many 'tagged' students' have simply been told at the end of their training that there is currently no employment available. If lucky, the given airline will prioritise them once recruitment recommences. I do not wish to be overly negative on this point, but the reader should be clear that a conditional offer of employment is NO GUARANTEE OF A JOB. It is precisely that – conditional on both the candidate passing training AND a position being available with the partner airline. This should be borne in mind when considering investing £100k+ in an integrated course.

The mechanics of an integrated course vary from provider to provider. The typical route starts with your Private Pilot Licence (PPL). You would then need to complete your Air Transport Pilot Licence (ATPL) theory ground school. The next steps are to hour build, achieve your night rating, complete your Multi-Engine Instrument Rating (MEIR) and then obtain your Commercial Pilot Licence (CPL). The final step is to complete your Multi-Crew Course (MCC) and Upset Prevention and Recovery Training (UPRT). I will explain in more detail what each of these stages comprise.

The point I want to make is on integrated courses is, although training up to the advanced stage of PPL is conducted, there is no PPL skills test on some integrated courses. Instead, those integrated courses will only test at CPL stage in a twin-engine aircraft. The carries the disadvantage to the student that they will not be allowed to hire a single-engine plane as a private pilot would. Why does this matter? If for whatever reason there are delays to your course, you will not be able to simply visit your local airfield to hire and fly aircraft on your own in order to remain current. The same applies after you have completed your training. If you want to fly a single-engine aircraft, you will have to undergo and pay for additional training.

There are some excellent integrated courses and in the next section I will share points that the reader should take into consideration when deciding which course to take. There are some excellent value integrated courses if you shop around. Look beyond the most prominent schools and, if your situation allows, it may be worth exploring courses in other European countries. A good question to ask when researching prospective schools is to ask where graduates have landed jobs at recently. Some integrated providers will say they will provide career placement assistance and place you in a 'hold pool'. When the industry is booming, people will get jobs anyway, but feedback from the experience of others who were offered this 'hold pool' opportunity was that the hold pool was very deep with waiting times of nine months plus. Also, the candidate may only be given one or a maximum of two opportunities for an assessment with an airline. If for example, a candidate was to be offered a position with airline X, but the location was just not suitable, the school may deem not accepting that job offer as inappropriate and remove the candidate from the hold pool.

While talking to another candidate during my airline assessment, I asked how they had been invited to the assessment; thinking they may have been offered it via their integrated course. I was surprised to learn that the candidate had applied and secured the interview without the flying school's help. When I asked if they had been given any other opportunities from the 'hold pool' the answer was that after nine months they had not been put forward. This candidate had paid £100k plus for their integrated course. I had spent around £60k on my modular course, yet there was no real difference when it came to the chances of securing a job. I have also met people who were offered an airline interview the same day they completed their pilot training. Hold pools are no guarantee of a suitable job offer and you need to be prepared to get out there and find a job yourself.

Now that I have shared a couple of the negatives about integrated courses, there are some integrated courses from good schools that are well priced that fall within the ballpark of what I paid for my modular training. A quick search on Google will reveal some options with some of these schools running accredited airline schemes. Ideally, when selecting an integrated course:

- The student will not be paying over the odds. Get several quotes and negotiate.
- The training standard and quality should be excellent. A good indicator will be the number of students gaining employment after the course. Ask for school feedback in online forums like www.pprune.org and the many Facebook groups that exist relating to pilot training.
- The flying school will have reasonable and honest management. You will have setbacks during your training, so it is essential to train with an organisation with whom you can work well. Ask past students of their experiences - PPRuNe & Facebook are good places to find opinions.

For the readers deciding to pursue an integrated course which requires an initial assessment, (this is to allow the school to determine if they will accept you on the course), the assessment process usually consists of some sort of aptitude testing. You can research your specific school to find out which type of aptitude testing takes place, e.g. CUT-E, ADAPT etc. You can also prepare for particular elements of the testing like mental arithmetic and verbal reasoning. These are available online and are worth doing. I also found it helpful to ask other candidates how they found their assessments online. PPRuNe is an excellent forum for this type of information. The next part of the evaluation is usually focused around a group exercise and HR interview. The key during the group exercise is to be a good team player, relax and participate. The environment is somewhat artificial but try your best. Do not allow yourself to be overpowered by more dominant members of the group and equally, do not dominate the task but allow others to participate. There are some strategies you can employ, for example, using a decision-making process like DODAR (Diagnosis, Options, Decision, Assessment, Revision). There will also typically be a competency/HR based interview to determine your motivation for wanting to participate in the course. To assist you in completion of your application and preparation for interviews, I have listed some useful resources on my blog at kcthepilot.com/book.

Multi Pilot Licence (MPL) Courses

The MPL course is a version of an integrated course that is focused purely on the airline environment. The licence to be gained at the end of the training can only be used in a multi-crew (needs more than one pilot) airline environment on the specific type of aircraft that the partner airline uses. The MPL licence as such could be much more restricting to anyone wanting to fly outside of the airline environment. In comparison, the traditional integrated route gives you a fATPL which provides more flexibility in the licence use. The point of the multi-pilot licence was to produce ab initio (zero experience) pilots to be able to go straight into the right-hand seat of a small airliner. The program is based on being trained in partnership with a specific airline using their procedures. Compared to the traditional integrated course route, the student on an MPL program would complete significantly less flying in an actual aircraft (around 80 hours vs circa 200 hours on a traditional path). However, the MPL student will spend a lot more time early in the programme, in a simulator working with the sponsoring airline's' procedures. The MPL student is a lot better suited for airline operations resulting from the high level of simulator time and training. Note that traditional integrated route students will require additional training via a 'type rating' course when they join an airline.

The argument for the MPL course is that most traditional pilot training used single-engine or multi-engine piston aircraft and had no real bearing on how a modern jetliner operates in a multi-crew environment. The MPL licence can only be issued after all training is complete and 12 take-off and landings have been flown in the sponsoring airline's aircraft type. The problem to consider is what would happen if the sponsor airline, for whatever reason, was not able to complete the final stage of training (12 take-off and landings in the aircraft), preventing the issuing the MPL licence. What would happen, if, during your training, the sponsoring airline realised that they no longer had a job for you due to lower demand for air travel? You would not be able to complete the 12 take-off and landings and you would not be able to obtain your MPL licence. Integrated courses take around 18 months and, of course, a lot can change during that time regarding the outlook and business environment of a given sponsoring airline.

During the COVID 19 outbreak, many airlines have scaled back their operations, letting many experienced pilots go. Airline fleet expansion plans have been delayed and this has meant that students in their MPL programs are for now, surplus to requirements. An MPL licence can be brought in line with the privileges of a fATPL, but that requires further training and testing. There is a clear path to convert your MPL licence once the training is complete. The worrying gap remains of what if midway during your MPL training, the partner airline goes bust or no longer needs you and your training is interrupted? There is no clear path of how to revert to the traditional fATPL training route without spending a lot of money. Effectively, a student can spend most of their £100k + and subsequently find that their airline doesn't need them. The MPL student is left with absolutely nothing (particularly if the 12 take-off and landings have not been completed). This is the risk that MPL students need to consider carefully, especially when committing such high costs for pilot training.

If the training has been financed through a loan, the repayments will still have to be made. How those repayments will be made is anyone's guess, especially as the student was expecting to be in a full-time employment in a First Officer position that is not going to happen anytime soon. For the student to convert to a traditional fATPL and pursue regular non-airline flying employment, for example via air survey, flying instructor, etc., there would be a high conversion cost. Assuming the MPL licence has been issued (12 take-offs and landing completed), the student would need to undertake a Commercial Pilot Licence (CPL) course. The lowest cost, including test fees, is around £8k-£9k. The student would then need to complete a Multi-Engine Instrument Rating (MEIR) for single-pilot use. There is some cross-credit available, but at the very least, the competency-based route would require fifteen hours in a twin aircraft plus test fee. This would probably cost another £10k minimum. I am not sure if a Multi-Crew Course (MCC) would be necessary. Still, if it was, then you can easily add another £7k-£9k bringing the total conversion cost to around £25k-£30k minimum to have the same privileges on the licence as a traditional route fATPL pilot.

I have no issues with the MPL licence concept and is an excellent idea with regards to focused training for the airline environment. However, I would suggest that at the moment, all the risk is with the student, the training organisation and sponsoring airline can walk away at any stage. If the risk is with the student, then at the very least, the student should have something in hand that represents the value paid, e.g. PPL, CPL etc. as provided through the traditional route. During my modular pilot training, I was very careful to 'bank the money as I went'. I made sure after any test that I sent the paperwork off the CAA at the earliest opportunity and I would gather all my flight school reports as soon as each phase of flight training was complete. For obvious reasons, I would be very wary of enrolling on any programme that costs over £100k without any qualification gained until right at the end. The recent MPL issues during COVID 19 should open peoples' eyes to the risk of some MPL programmes. Traditional training programmes are not without risk either, but at least with regular route pilot training, 'you bank your money' as you go and can make use of your licence outside of the commercial airline environment if things do not work out.

As I mentioned at the start of this guide, many years ago, I was declined for an integrated MPL programme. The reason given was that I did not show enough captaincy during the group exercises. To the aspiring pilot there is usually a good reason for a wall appearing in your path, although the reason may not be obvious at the time. For me, being turned down for the MPL program was probably one of the best things that could have happened to me. It pushed me down the modular route and I was able to complete my training at a much lower cost and in a significantly shorter timeframe. Being able to continue working, I could also protect my earnings at the same time.

Modular Pilot Training

We will now consider modular training. This has its benefits in that you can carry out your training at a pace that suits you and your cash flow, provided the various time limits and expiry dates of certain aspects of the training are respected. You are not tied to any one particular training organisation. The downside is you have to motivate yourself. It can also be quite an isolating experience especially as, for the bulk of the time, you will be on your own without the camaraderie you would typically have with a full-time integrated course where you get to bond with your course mates. I enjoyed the self-funded modular route as, despite the isolation, it worked out well for me. I was able to keep my full-time job while continuing my flight training. Although not particularly well advertised in the flying school community, a key point to note is once your training is complete, it costs even more to secure employment (more on this below).

The typical modular path would be for the student to complete their PPL and then enrol onto an ATPL theory class. ATPL theory can either be on a full-time or distance learning basis. There is no hard and fast rule to dictate which path is better; just do what works best for you and your situation at the time. I was working full time and needed my job to help fund my training, so the only solution for me was an ATPL theory distance learning course. Other people I have spoken to struggle to motivate themselves to work in isolation and preferred the full-time classroom environment. After completing the ATPL theory exams the student would then continue with their hour building and night rating. A decision then needs to be made on where to tackle the CPL and Multi-Engine Instrument Rating

(MEIR). The final part of the modular training is the Multi-Crew Course (MCC) and Advanced Upset Prevention and Recovery Training (UPRT). The CPL & MEIR & MCC element all-in cost around £25-£50k depending on where and how the training is completed. To complete the CPL + MEIR + MCC element on a full-time basis, one would need to set aside around four months. It can be completed a little faster, but it can also take a lot longer if the weather is not favourable. I did my CPL & MEIR part-time during the weekends only and took around six months to complete. You want to do as much of your flying as possible in the months when the weather is good. In later chapters, I will speak more about some of the problems that I had during training and some of the challenges associated with completing my flight training in 12 months with while holding down a full-time job.

Setbacks

My original training path was to apply for an integrated MPL Course based on the conditional provision of employment by an airline. As mentioned earlier, I reached the final stage of the assessment but was unsuccessful. Via the modular route, I still completed my training and secured employment with a major airline flying the Boeing 737. During my multi-crew course and line assessments (once in the job), my teamwork and leadership were scored as being very good and the comment had been made that I showed good command potential. The modular path worked out much better for me as I completed my flight training at approximately 40% less cost than what the integrated course would have cost.

Furthermore, my failure to pass the integrated MPL course and 'assessed as being a weak leader' made no bearing on my subsequent ability to secure a job. It makes you wonder how reliable airline assessments are at such an early stage. I guess the recruiters need some way of whittling down the vast number of applicants. My advice is to take the assessment feedback on board, but don't give it too much weight. People have passed integrated course assessments with flying colours and subsequently struggled during their pilot training and finding line training difficult once in the airline. Then there are people like me, who were assessed as not meeting the required standard but have through proper training, still succeeded and achieved the required standard. Don't give up, even if the first few answers are "no". I guess the other part of the equation that needs to be addressed is at what point do you give up if unfortunately, you just don't have the temperament and ability to fly? I do not have the perfect answer, but I would suggest stopping somewhere before you start spending serious money on flight training that you may not use. For some people this may be after a few PPL lessons. For others it may be completing their PPL and flying for leisure, but not going any further than that.

When is the right time to start your training?

We are currently in the middle of the COVID-19 crisis with the airline industry in turmoil. Many people are discouraging pilot training on the basis that a lot of more experienced pilots are currently unemployed. I get that and understand that in short to medium term, there is very little by way of employment opportunity. That said, I think the question you should now be asking is 'when would be the right time to start training'. If someone had taken the advice to start their training 18 months before the COVID 19 crisis when everyone in the industry was projecting astronomical growth (airlines, aeroplane manufacturers etc.), they would have completed their training and found little pilot employment opportunities. Can anyone be relied upon to advise on the correct time to start flight training is? The answer is nobody knows what can happen tomorrow. What

I have found to be consistent though is people tend to be overly optimistic in the good times and too pessimistic after a shock event. The important thing is to have a backup plan in case you do not find a flying job immediately.

My approach to flight training was that I already had a full-time job, so I was not under any real pressure to secure a pilot job. I loved flying and knew I would thoroughly enjoy my flight training come what may. If it led to an airline job, great, but if it hadn't, I would be more than happy, for example, instructing during the weekend as a hobby. Without any real expectation of what would come at the end of my modular pilot journey, I took each step at a time and just enjoyed my flying. When I did eventually finish my training the airline industry was very buoyant and many of us were getting over three job offers in quick succession. It worked out for me. I guess you have to ask yourself the question of what will your position be if you cannot secure employment. Will it lead to financial ruin? Will you be happy and content with the experiences? If the outcome of your analysis is that you have to secure an airline job at the end of it or you will run into severe financial difficulty from all the debt, then it is probably not a good idea to be so highly leveraged. It may make more sense to space your training out and pay for it as you go without having to accumulate so much debt.

I always used to say to myself, 'I want to fly professionally, but not at any financial cost'. I urge the reader to consider this carefully. In my case, I first flew an aircraft in the air cadets at 14 years old and it was not until a week before my 34th birthday that I flew a Boeing 737 for the first time. During that time, we had 9/11, the financial crisis (x2), SARS, terror attacks and multiple airlines going bankrupt (Monarch, Flybe, Thomas Cook, Primera, the list goes on). The aviation industry will always be up and down and it is impossible to predict what will happen. Rather than try to forecast and time your training, try approaching it from a different angle. Pursue aviation for the pleasure of it (without bankrupting yourself) and just enjoy yourself. If a job comes along - great, if it doesn't, make sure your life is arranged in such a way that the show can still go on. Although there will be periodic slumps in air travel, demand always comes back (eventually). In times of crisis airlines will freeze and stop recruiting altogether. As the training pipeline is almost always abruptly cut off, in the subsequent upturn, there is an inevitable shortage of crew. These sharp swings in pilot recruitment create opportunity as existing pilots reach retirement age; eventually, expansion returns and new planes are ordered. For those that have the right paperwork and happen to be in the right place, there will ultimately be a job opportunity.

Chapter 5: Private Pilot Licence (PPL)

I did my PPL training ten years ago and there has been no real structural change to the training or how the PPL is taught and tested in that time. The training consists of a minimum of 45 hours instruction, of which a minimum 25 hours of those have to be dual (you and the instructor) and a minimum of 10 hours of supervised solo. As part of the flying you have to complete a solo qualifying cross-country flight of 150NM (270km) round trip landing at two different airfields from the one of departure. The qualifying cross country flight is a significant milestone for any PPL student. You are also required to complete nine theoretical exams in a range of subjects ranging from air law to meteorology.

As it has been a while since I did my PPL, I am referring back to my logbook as I write this. The first thing that is apparent is the intensity of my flying. One of the pieces of advice I would give to the reader (and I will repeat this advice throughout the guide) is that you do not want to do pilot training 'slowly'. Pilot training is expensive enough as it is and if your lessons are spread out too far apart, you will find that you have to keep re-learning lessons, which will increase your costs. When planning your training, this is a consideration you need to apply in terms of when you start your flight training and maintaining a reasonable pace. It's helpful to have your ducks in a row (money and time), in order to concentrate on progressing your flight training. As I was working at my job Monday to Friday I would typically book in for my PPL lessons on Saturday and Sunday. My PPL training was based around having a lesson in the morning, taking a break and then having another lesson in the afternoon on both Saturday and Sunday. I repeated this pattern for my subsequent flying courses (CPL & IR). This intensity of lessons may be a bit much if you are new to flying and you may find one lesson a day is enough. I had been racing in gliders previously with some of my flights lasting more than five hours and so had a reasonable amount of 'match fitness' already.

For your PPL there is a certain amount of equipment that you will need to buy. On my website page to support this guide; kcthepilot.com/book, I have listed the resources and tactics that may help you save some money on this equipment. For PPL you want your cash to be going into hours in the air, not fancy gear. As with any other learning process, try to be as organised as possible when it comes to flying lessons. This includes making sure you have all your equipment ready for when its needed and ensuring that you are in a fit state to operate.

The flight training world is a peculiar place. In one sense, you are a paying customer for a given service at the flying school and would expect yourself to be treated that way. However, you also have to manage your instructor as your customer as, effectively, they are going to decide whether or not you pass your PPL. I can hear you saying "surely the instructor wouldn't be allowed to be my PPL examiner!" However, during your PPL training, your flying instructor will spend around 50-60 hours flying with you and is, therefore, in a good position to assess your competence. Although you have a standard lesson, you are in effect, undergoing a 'skills test' with each lesson. I appreciate that there is no hard pass or fail criteria for each lesson, but remember it is your PPL instructor who will have a significant say as to whether or not you are put forward for the test. The CAA examiner who does eventually carry out your PPL skills test is there effectively in a 'quality control' capacity and relying on your flight instructor to have made the right judgment call that you are ready. The CAA examiner will only fly with you for around

2 hours and will not have anything like the same depth of information as that compiled by your regular flying instructor.

Back to equipment then as we try to build a picture to our instructor that we are reliable and well organised. The first item for discussion is a headset. Pre COVID-19, I would have said a headset is not necessary, as you can borrow one from the flying school. However, while COVID-19 is still prevalent, I would say a personal headset is an essential item. At PPL level, there is no need to buy an expensive headset. A budget one will do. If, later on, you are sure you will be flying commercially and spending 12 hours a day on your headset in an aircraft, then fine, go ahead and invest in a higher quality headset.

The next must-have is your PPL books – electronic or hard copy – do what works best for your style of learning. I still have my manuals on my bookshelf to this day as I like referring back to them now and then. One of the manuals (Air Pilot's Manual - Flying Training) focuses on each of the flying lessons and exercises you will be undertaking. I used to ask the instructor what we would be working on for the next lessons in the week and would read ahead. Reading ahead will save you time (and money in the air) and gives you a chance to absorb information as things happen fast in the air. Throughout your pilot training, the more you do on the ground on your sofa, in your kitchen or even practising your checks in the car, the more comfortable life is in the air.

You will also need a flight case, fine permanent markers for your map and a navigation set. A navigation set is a ruler, plotter, protractor etc. – all the items you need to draw on your map and a plog (Navigation log). A plog is flying speak for the table you fill in before flying with your waypoints, distances, track information etc. and have on your kneeboard to conduct the flight.

Flight calculators. Depending on how far you want to take your flying (if commercial) you will need one of the more expensive versions of a flight calculator. If sticking to PPL, you will be okay with one of the lower-cost versions that does not have all the functionally needed for CPL. I am deliberately not going into specific makes and models as times change, and products evolve. Ask your instructor or have a look at my website, which I will try to keep as up to date as possible. You will also need a stopwatch – a cheap plastic one is perfect. Don't forget your maps and charts for the area and places you will be flying in. Your flying school will have maps for sale, or you can buy them online. Finally, you will need a logbook and a high-visibility vest or jacket. Speak to your instructor or flight school about a checklist and if it is necessary to buy one. Some flying schools have their own approved checklists that they use. Others use commercially available options.

The next aspect the PPL to consider is the nine ground school exams. On the whole PPL ground school is very manageable with very little of it causing difficulty provided you have GCSE level maths and physics. Some of the study tools you can use to assist you include question banks (practice questions- there are many apps available) Facebook groups and the wealth of information freely available on YouTube. The key to your PPL ground school is work steadily through and if you are struggling, ask for help from your instructor. For the nine PPL ground school exams, doing my training in the UK, I would always go to the airfield if I had a lesson booked even if the weather is not flyable. The rainy days would be spent completing my PPL ground school and exams. The rainy-day tactic works as we get a lot of wet days in the UK!

The flying is split into 19 exercises which you need to master to complete the PPL skills test. The flying manuals cover this area much better than I could ever wish to, but the main thing I would add is that at times it will feel overwhelming and at first you will wonder if you will ever be able to pass your PPL test. As with any new skill, with repeated practice, the less you need to think about what you are doing, the more your capacity grows. Remember the first few driving lessons you had where you were focused on the next event (change gear, indicate, steer around the corner, etc.). The more time spent driving, the more you can 'see ahead' and, in effect, can predict when a problem might occur. You subconsciously plan much more and are much more aware of other road users. The same thing will happen on your PPL. You start off being consumed by just flying the aircraft: maintaining a heading or a given altitude, but as time progresses you don't think about the basics, they become automatic and your capacity grows to be able to manage the flight and plan ahead.

CHAPTER 6: HOUR BUILDING

With your PPL complete, the next step is to make a start on your hour building. How you approach your hour building will make or break your CPL course. Although this chapter is focused on hour building, I will send most of it sharing how you can prepare for your CPL course during hour building. Hour building is an incredible time for any pilot during their training. There will not be many times in your life when you can simply jump into an aircraft and fly halfway across the country to get some fish and chips! Enjoy your hour building, but do not lose sight of the reason why you are doing it. An excellent approach to hour building is to think of it as preparation for your commercial pilot licence. You can download my PPL/CPL hour building app with the link available at kcthepilot.com/ppl-cpl-hour-building-app. The app offers suggestions for items to work on during the various stages of your hour building to make your hour building more structured.

An excellent book to read early on during your hour building is 'a guide to the EASA CPL test flight'. This book illustrates how your CPL skills test will work and in turn, allows you to see the techniques you need to master beforehand. It will be to your advantage to arrive on your CPL course already proficient in the areas you can practice on your own. This will free up capacity during the CPL course to focus on the things which are new to you or where you may have weaknesses. The significant difference between PPL and CPL flying is formality and captaincy. You do not have to wait until your CPL course to start working on these skills. You can practice and become proficient beforehand. I have provided a list of exercises to work on within my app.

From the formality perspective, the big difference between PPL and CPL is getting to grips with aircraft documentation. During PPL the flying school would most likely have taken care of this for you. However, although you have a PPL, you need to start thinking like a commercial pilot undertaking public transport - the buck stops with you as the commander. If, during your hour building, you approach each day like you are conducting a public transport flight, this should help ease your path through your CPL course.

The first part of approaching hour building with 'CPL mindset' is to verify you have complete aircraft documents. Check the certificate of registration. The certificate of registration is non-expiring. The aircraft documents should also contain the following:

- certificate of airworthiness (valid unless revoked)
- airworthiness review certificate (1-year validity)
- noise certificate
- aircraft radio licence
- mass and balance and a certificate of insurance (valid for 1 year).

I appreciate that we are only at the hour building stage right now, so why do I keep referring to the CPL course? Well, to make the most of your hour building, it is critical to work back from the CPL requirements and spend the time practising, as much as you can, what will come up on your CPL course. Enjoy hour building, just don't lose focus of the end goal - that is to be as prepared for your CPL course as possible. If you get into the habit of aspiring to achieve CPL standard pre-flight preparation during your hour building, it will make life so much easier on your CPL course. Your hour building will also be much safer as you will be less likely to get into trouble in the air from poor pre-flight preparation.

With the reader now armed with the knowledge of approaching hour building as if on a CPL course, there are some of the items to consider. When you arrive at your CPL course and test it is expected that your pre-flight preparation includes actual flight planning with a marked map and plog. Keep practising this skill during your hour building. During CPL you will be expected to have calculated and completed mass and balance for all phases of flight and the examiner will also expect a weather brief. The weather information must come from official sources (not SkyDemon). Your examiner will also expect to be briefed on pertinent Notice to Airmen (NOTAMs). You can use electronic tools to assist with your pre-flight planning, but that should not be at the expense of getting the information from official sources. Using electronic sources to assist you with your flight planning can be helpful and save time. For example, it is much easier to see where a given NOTAM is when it is illustrated on a map rather than trying to visualise grid coordinates. During my CPL test, I used SkyDemon to place temporary airspace restrictions on my map but still printed off the NOTAMs from the official source. The more time you spend practising and making a habit of conducting this level of preparation for each flight during hour building, the easier your life will be at CPL stage.

The next part of the hour building element is to get to know your aircraft. Very few pilots read the Pilot Operating Handbook (POH) for their respective aircraft. Although your CPL course will probably be on a different aircraft type to that which you are hour building; it is still a very worthwhile exercise. For starters, during one of my airline assessments, the company was known to ask questions about your previous aircraft types. If you had not read your POH, you would struggle to answer these questions. If you had read the POH; this is an easy tick in the box to get the interviewer on side during a technical interview. The items that are typically asked are not challenging, for example: What voltage is the electrical system in your aircraft? Describe the electrical system? What is the fuel consumption of your aircraft? This leads to the next stage of the assessment: the walk-around of the aircraft. During your CPL test, the examiner will expect you to complete your walk-around by following the POH. I appreciate that we all develop our style of doing things but, during CPL, it is critical to do everything by the book. If your examiner wanted to be pedantic, they are well within their rights to follow you around the aircraft doing your walk around. If the inspection is not by the book you can quickly be wrong-footed for the rest of your test. It is much easier to develop good habits early instead of having to make significant behavioural corrections after 100 hours of hour building.

We now move onto the taxi and take off. Again, I advise that you stay disciplined and get used to doing the checks out aloud. Although you may be able to perform these in your head, the only way the examiner will know you are doing the checks correctly is if you verbalise them. It is standard practice for the examiner to have a copy of the approved checklist and follow you through should they so wish. Very few PPL pilots bother with performance calculations as for the majority of the time they are operating from airfields with much more runway than needed. Whether this is the case or not, practice your performance calculations periodically, so you don't forget how to do them.

Continue to work on your aerodrome and traffic pattern operation including different joins. Although CPL is based around taking the most expeditious route, be comfortable joining airfields from overhead, downwind, long base and also long finals. This brings me to my next point, which is the lookout. Do not to get too relaxed on this and keep working hard to look outside. Lookout is paramount for collision avoidance. During PPL you would have spent most of your time on QNH (sea level pressure). Hour building will be the first time that you may use a flight level. Discipline with altimeter setting procedures is not only a CPL requirement, but it will keep you alive and stop you crashing into terrain.

The hour building app gives a concise to-do list designed to encourage working on those items that may not ordinarily be covered when hour building. During hour building it is very worthwhile to periodically spend an hour or two with an instructor, say every 25-30 hours. This will provide an excellent opportunity to obtain valuable feedback, especially if any bad habits have developed, which can be caught early. Flying with an instructor will also allow you to practice some of the PPL instructor-led exercises such as stalls, spiral dives, engine failures and fires and to practice forced landings. If you are doing your CPL course on a single-engine aircraft, these will be covered on the CPL course and during your test.

While you are exploring various airfields, keep in mind to be disciplined with fuel planning and maintaining an accurate fuel plog. If you are not sure how, ask your instructor. For CPL your basic navigation skills need to be good. Although I used electronic maps during my hour building, I always made a point of plotting a map and having a plog for my flights for the day. I used the electronic aids as a backup and built confidence in what I was doing manually with a map, compass and stopwatch. It is essential to remain practised with diversions and diversion management too. The more comfortable you are with conventional navigation, the easier your CPL course will be. I saw a post on one of the forums from a student complaining that during a CPL course navigation flight the instructor had asked them to find a takeaway shop in the middle of Birmingham! Hopefully, your examiner is not as brutal as that, but in any case, the diversion target on your test will be small and probably not the easiest to find. You need to be confident in your navigation, and a lot of that will depend on how you spend your hour building with regards challenging yourself to find obscure places during hour building and practising diversions.

When you are planning your hour building flights, try and set an objective for each flight that will make you feel slightly uncomfortable. Do not do anything unsafe or illegal. If you are not 100% confident on the radio for example, keep forcing yourself to transit controlled airspace. With enough practise the weakness will become a strength. During my hour building, I completed an Instrument Meteorological Conditions Rating (IMC), so I was comfortable working the navigation aids. Keep practising your PPL instrument navigation as during your CPL test you will need to track VOR/NDBs and fix your position using navigation aids. The CPL is challenging (I thought it was the hardest part of flight training) but you can achieve a first-time pass. You just have to work hard and much of the outcome for CPL depends on how much capacity you developed during hour building. If you have spent your time on challenging flights, going in and out of controlled airspace, keeping the discipline etc., then CPL and your Instrument Rating (IR) will be less stressful as the learning curve will not be as steep. For your IR, although you cannot do instrument flying during hour building unless you have a suitable rating, confidence on the radio will help you a lot. Going in and out of controlled airspace will increase your workload and as a result, your capacity, standing you in good stead for IR.

During your hour building, even when the weather is not great, there is still plenty that can be achieved. For mediocre days (still suitable for flying but not good enough to go a long distance), use the time to work on your circuits.

Practise some of the manoeuvres you wouldn't ordinarily complete, e.g. go-arounds, crosswind landings and short-field landings etc.

While you are enjoying your hour building and having fun, if the opportunity arises and conditions safely allow, try and plan a flight to a different country or a few trips that require you to file a flight plan such as crossing a Flight Information Region (FIR) boundary.

At some stage during your hour building you will need to complete your 300NM CPL qualifying cross country. The following are points that should be considered to improve your chances of a successful outcome:

- Select airfields close to the coast and of lower elevation. If the cloud base is slow to lift, higher elevation airfields will take longer to clear up.
- Although you do not want to do anything unsafe or illegal, try not to wait for the 'perfect day'. The chances are you will probably never get a perfect day. Try and set off early. On my CPL qualifier, my route was Blackpool > Tatenhill > Duxford > Blackpool. When I set off for Tatenhill on my first leg, the weather at Duxford was out of limits and supposed to clear up. I planned that once I got to Tatenhill I would check the Duxford weather. If the weather was still not suitable, I would abandon the qualifier attempt and return to Blackpool. Thankfully, by the time I had got to Tatenhill, the weather had cleared up in Duxford. If I had waited in Blackpool until the Duxford weather was suitable, it would have been too late in the day to set off.
- Try and minimise the unknowns or 'new' things on the day. I visited Duxford and Tatenhill individually on different days beforehand. Simple things like

knowing where to pay your landing fee or how to order fuel can save a lot of stress on the day.

However you decide to complete your hour building you will need to have access to an aircraft for whenever you need it. Ideally it needs to be available all day for maximum flexibility. Some people purchase their own plane. Others join a group or no equity scheme. A no equity scheme is similar to buying a share in an aircraft, except there is no upfront purchase fee and you just pay a monthly fixed amount for access to the plane and an hourly fee per hour you fly. I found the flying school aircraft hire worked well for me as my flying club was never short of aircraft. While you do not want to annoy your colleagues by booking a plane for a whole day and only fly for an hour in the morning, you can increase your progress and success during hour building if you have access to an aircraft whenever you need it. Operating in the flying school environment can be challenging as you do not know what the weather will do and you do not want to be sat on the ground wasting time waiting for the aircraft to come back from someone else's lesson on a glorious day. Figure out what is most economical and works best for you between aircraft purchase, no equity scheme or flying school hire.

CHAPTER 7: AIR TRANSPORT PILOT LICENCE (ATPL) THEORY

At some stage after PPL you will need to complete your 14 ATPL theory exams. If you happen to be on an integrated course this phase of your flight training may occur at the very first stage of your course before you complete any flying. If not on an integrated course, you have to wait until you have a PPL before starting your ATPL Theory. If, like me, you progress down the modular route, you may find the natural time to complete your ATPLs is during hour building. Some people prefer to focus purely on the ATPLs and then pursue hour building afterwards. Others prefer to complete their hour building then start the ATPLs. Either will work, but generally what drives the decision are your present circumstances in terms of how comfortable you feel juggling hour building with ATPL study. The time of year may also inform your decision. In wintertime hour building will naturally be slower due to the weather so this may be the time to better focus on the ATPL theory.

The next question that needs to be answered is what type of course should you enrol upon to complete your ATPL theory. Your learning style and personal circumstances will drive how you complete your studies. There are full-time and part-time alternatives. Some people prefer to be in a full-time classroom environment and enjoy mixing it with fellow course mates. I was constrained by the need to work full time; therefore, the only alternative for me was to proceed via distance learning. Whichever route you choose there are a few questions to ask:

- How much does the course costs? Many providers like to advertise attention-grabbing prices only for you to find out once you enrol that you need to pay extra for course materials, access to certain information etc.

- Ask students who are currently undertaking ATPL theory feedback on the given institution via Facebook ATPL groups.
- Where study is via distance learning there is a certain amount of mandatory 'classroom time'. I did my ATPL theory with a provider called CATS Aviation in the UK. Their course involved four compulsory classroom days to brush up ready for the exams for each of the three modules. Different providers work differently, so find the one that works best for your circumstances.

The ATPL theory exams are not demanding in terms of technical content, however, the volume of information and concepts with which you need to become comfortable can be demanding. The key to getting through your ATPL theory is to be consistent with the amount you study each day or per week and grind through. Get into a study routine and stick to it. I set myself a target of 3 hours of study per day and, as I was working full-time, I would set my alarm for 4:30 am and try and do a few hours before work. At lunchtime, with the course content on my iPad, I would do another 30 minutes or so. When I got home in the evening, I would then do another 30 minutes to an hour. I would then go to bed early, ready to repeat the process. Find what works for you and get into a pattern. ATPL theory takes at least six months on a full-time course. Although I completed mine in 8 months it was quite intense. You must take regular, decent sized breaks from your studies and avoid the risk of burning out. My break was on Saturday and Sunday. I made sure I did no study during the weekend. Hour building during the weekend helped as it put purpose to all the crazy study during the week and, having fun in the air, allowed me to unwind and relax.

The question does come up regularly of how relevant ATPL theory is to actual commercial flying in the real world. Some of it is not relevant. Other parts of it are useful. The highlight subject that I found of immediate use was meteorology. In particular, the aspects relating to frontal weather systems and being able to look at a synoptic chart and build a picture of what the weather is doing. ATPL meteorology helped me during my hour building and I continue to use a lot of the performance, navigation and flight planning elements at work flying the Boeing 737. Although we have electronic tools to streamline some of the processes, it is still essential to understand what is going on behind all of the automated tools. ATPL theory is tough, but work consistently and remain disciplined and you will get through.

A key area suffering from neglect in my view, is the provision of guidance on how to study. This becomes more acute if you have been out of education for a while. I did not place particular importance on this side of things until I stumbled across a book 'Unlimited Memory' by Kevin Horsley. This encouraged me to put together an online class on how to study effectively. Check it out in the resources section of kcthepilot.com/book. The process I thought made the most sense was to start with answering:

- Why do you want to become a pilot? Once you have a solid reason for wanting to do so (beyond 'it looks cool'), then the next stages become much easier to achieve.
- How do we eliminate distractions and find a suitable workspace?
- We need to have a plan for how we will conduct our studies. An elite runner does not randomly go out for runs in the hope of winning world championships. The same should apply to us. We need to have a long-term plan of how we will reach

our objective then break that down into individual day to day, hour to hour activities.

With a good plan we can now commence studying. A lot of people rush to memorise facts without truly understanding what is behind those facts. Not fully understanding a subject will impede your ability to transfer the information to memory as it has no relevance. I found the Feynman technique works best to understand a concept or information. The Feynman technique is based upon:

1) Choose an idea to learn about.
2) Try and explain the idea to someone with no knowledge or understanding of the subject you are talking about.
3) Identify the gaps in your knowledge.
4) Revisit the information and simplify it and try again!

It is only when we correctly understand the information that we can then look to place it into our memory. Unfortunately, most people don't realise how weak the traditional techniques can be in active memory recall, e.g. writing something down over and over again until it sticks. There are much more efficient ways to store items to memory, and the book Unlimited Memory helps. If you are interested, do have a look in the resources section kcthepilot.com/book

Once you have understood and learnt the concept, the next step is to practice recalling the information. This is where the questions banks come into play. Question banks are an online resource of past exam-style questions based on student feedback after they have sat exams. The tactic I adopted to complete a given subject would be to try to reach the stage where all the material was covered and understood around six weeks before the exam. I would then spend the remaining six weeks practising questions and going over areas where gaps had materialised. I found that this practice helped for subjects that required a certain speed of execution, for example, general navigation and flight planning. I remember doing my first general navigation and flight planning mock tests where I failed to get beyond 20% of the way through the exam within the allotted time. With lots and lots of practice with the question bank my speed improved until, after a few weeks, I managed to complete an exam within the allotted time. The next step was to try to move my average score in a given exam from 50% up towards the 100% mark. This again takes time and more practice and revisiting study material. It can be done - don't give up!

Another complication with ATPLs is that once you have sat your first exam you are time-limited. After sitting your first exam all 14 exams have to be completed within 18 months. You also have a maximum of six 'sittings' to complete all 14. A sitting is considered a series of bookings for ATPL exams in a particular week. A final point to note is that employers pay attention to the number of attempts you took to pass a given subject. The goal is to achieve a first-time pass in all topics.

The odd re-sit is unlikely to hamper your chances of securing employment. However, that being said, when you do go for an interview for a professional pilot role, you are trying to build a picture of not being a training (and therefore, cost) risk. An easy win during the interview process is to have a home run of first time ATPL exam passes. For this reason, I would advise you do not sit any exams until you are convinced you are ready. I don't think anyone ever goes into an exam feeling 100% confident, but there is a difference between being cautiously optimistic after lots of hard work and preparing well versus not having done enough work and hoping 'it will be alright on the night'. Only you will know if you are ready or not. The airline jobs market is extremely competitive (particularly for low hour pilots) and messing up your ATPL theory is a sure way to exclude yourself from the market. There is not much more to say about ATPL theory other than do not lose sight of the end goal - it won't last forever, just grind through.

CHAPTER 8: NIGHT RATING AND IMC RATING

At some stage during your hour building, you will need to complete your night rating. The night rating is one of the fun parts of your flight training, as there is little pressure by way of any written exams or flight tests. The night rating is all completed in the aircraft. The night rating is a 5-hour course that consists of some dual instruction at night (including cross-country flight) and some solo work. I did my night rating in the longer nights of the winter. The most challenging aspect of the night rating is finding a weather window to complete the training.

In the UK, we do occasionally get those cold, crisp and still winter evenings. The night rating helped me with my hour building as it meant that I could conduct longer flights without worrying about running out of daylight when the weather was suitable. The airfield I used for hour building (Blackpool) was open until late and fully lit throughout the winter. Night Flying by R.D. Campbell is an excellent book which helped me through my night rating. Although the book was written some time ago the lessons are all still very relevant, from simple, common-sense tips like bringing a torch in your flight case to advice on in-flight emergencies at night. It is a very worthwhile read.

One of the items I had not appreciated that will assist you in your night rating is revising your instrument scan lessons from PPL. A good instrument scan will help your night rating (even though the night rating is a VFR course (visual flight rules - relying on looking outside).

Instrument Rating (Restricted)

One of the things that I did during my hour building was to complete an Instrument Meteorological Conditions (IMC) rating or Instrument Rating (Restricted). The IMC rating is a UK specific rating that allows a private pilot to fly in visibility down to 1800m and fly precision and non-precision approaches with the advice being to add 200ft to your Minimum Descent Altitude (MDA) or Decision Height (DH). The course itself is 15 hours and is designed to teach the student how to fly on instruments.

There are differing opinions on what and how this rating is to be used. Some people say it is a 'get you out of trouble' rating i.e. do not deliberately go flying in IMC, but keep it in your back pocket for when you inadvertently need it. There is another train of thought which is to be able to use the ratings safely, you need to remain practised, so challenge yourself and go flying when it is safe to do so but when the conditions are sub-optimal. I tended to sit somewhere in the middle. My primary concern was that in a single-engine piston aircraft if I had an engine failure, I wanted sufficient cloud base and visibility to be able to carry out a forced landing safely. Although theoretically with the rating, you could go flying with a cloud base of 300' and 1800m visibility. In an engine failure case, I did not feel I had a good enough answer to 'what was my plan if I had an engine failure?'. I did use the privilege of the rating regularly, but would only do so if the cloud base was high enough that in the event of an instrument or engine failure, I could still complete a landing visually. I would typically target a cloud base of at least 800'.

However you decide to use an IMC rating, make sure you are practised and have a plan for an instrument or engine failure. An appreciation of the much higher workload for single-pilot Instrument Flight Rules (IFR) is also crucial. I got my IMC rating almost by mistake. I undertook the IMC rating because I had booked some time off work for hour building, but the weather was abysmal for the week I had booked off. Rather than waste the time, I went ahead and did the IMC rating. An advantage of having an IMC rating is that it opens the door to a slightly shorter multi-engine instrument rating course via the competency-based instrument rating route. The standard instrument rating is a 55-hour course or 45 hours if you have a CPL.

If you meet specific requirements if previous IMC flight time (which the IMC rating provides), the competency-based route is a minimum of 15 hours provided you have the required experience. To be able to take advantage of any shortcut provided by the competency-based instrument rating route, you must ensure your IMC rating course includes a Basic Instrument Flight Module (with certificate) and that it is taught by an Instrument Rating Instructor (IRI). Using the competency-based instrument rating route I ended up needing 52 hours to get my full instrument rating, but still saved a bit of time compared to doing the full instrument rating. The real benefit from the IMC rating came during my hour building as I was able to exploit the marginal weather non-VFR days and get some flying done. The critical thing to bear in mind at all times is to remain safe and legal.

How did my costs compare doing an IMC rating then upgrading via the competency-based IR versus standard instrument rating? I spent more in total compared to what I would have just doing the standard Multi-Engine Instrument Rating course. Would I do the same again? Absolutely, because of the flexibility the IMC rating gave me during hour building to fly in marginal weather. The one thing to bear in mind for those considering doing an IMC rating then going via the competency-based instrument rating (CBIR), is the process only works if you have a lot of

IMC time. If you have not done much flying in IMC in the run-up to your competency-based instrument rating course, the CBIR can end up being more expensive in the long run. The reason for this is that the structure of the competency-based instrument rating is not as well defined compared to the standard instrument rating course. In the competency-based case, the instructor is expecting you to turn up with 'a level of competency' and patch up the gaps to reach the required standard. To make the CBIR route work you need to have done a reasonable amount of IMC flying. When I started my competency-based instrument rating, I had 20 hours in actual IMC – 15 hours from my IMC rating course and the rest from my hour building. I was very current and even then, was just borderline (having enough IMC experience) to benefit from the shorter CBIR course versus undertaking the full instrument rating.

A Basic Instrument Flight Module (BIFM) is a requirement for the CPL and IR course. If you do the IMC rating with a Basic Instrument Flight module, then you won't have to do it again during your CPL or IR courses. The critical aspect is to make sure your IMC rating includes a Basic Instrument Flight Module (within the approved training for the school - and don't forget your BIFM certificate!)

If doing an IMC or full instrument rating, I found the purchase of an electronic flight bag useful. My electronic flight bag consisted of an iPad mini that I could mount close to the instrument panel. For software, I downloaded Foreflight with a Jeppesen subscription for my charts and plates. All in, this was about £1000. Although expensive, having a moving map with IFR charts superimposed improved my situational awareness. It also meant that if I was hour building and conditions deteriorated to IMC, it was straightforward to get the relevant plates up on the screen. With the auto-update feature of the app I never had to worry about plates being out of date. Having an electronic flight bag means you also have access to all of the flight planning information you need (if you get the 4g iPad). You are not at the mercy of needing Wi-Fi and I liked being able to look after myself irrespective of the airfield I was visiting.

CHAPTER 9: MULTI-ENGINE INSTRUMENT RATING (MEIR)

With your hour building complete, the next stage is to work on your commercial pilot licence and move on to your instrument rating.

If you are taking the modular route there is no hard requirement for either of instrument rating (IR) or CPL to be completed in a particular order. In my case I started with IR on a part-time basis via the competency-based route. Juggling work and pilot training I needed to take full advantage of any longish duration holidays that I could get from work and get the most out of them. The company that I was working for at the time had a mandatory shut down period during Christmas, which gave me around ten days free for flight training. I wanted to fit in some flight training during that period and the most obvious choice for me to progress was my Multi-Engine Piston (MEP) rating. The MEP rating is a pre-requisite to your MEIR.

The MEP course is incredible for the pilot who has only been flying single-engine aircraft. The performance change to being in a twin aircraft is unforgettable. There are other key differences such as the aircraft having a retractable undercarriage and, with having two engines, the course soon starts to look at asymmetric flight (engine failure case). I thoroughly enjoyed the course but was faced with some challenges of which you should be aware. When selecting your pilot training school, one of the essential aspects you want to ask about is booking stability and aircraft and instructor availability. Early during my course, I was told one of my flying days would be cancelled as another student needed the plane for a test. While I had no problem with allowing the other student to take the aircraft, non-availability of either aircraft and instructor can play havoc with your training and progress. The lack of stability with my aircraft and instructor bookings continued to be a recurring theme through my MEP and IR training. To avoid making the same mistake with all the associated stress, be careful with flight school selection, as once you start a course, it is costly to start again with another.

The MEP course did have a theoretical element which was provided through the flying school. Reading the pilot operating handbook for the specific aircraft you will be flying will assist in some way.

On completion of the six-hour course you are not required to take your MEP skills test right away. The MEP skills test can be completed as part of your instrument rating skills test. I was paranoid about the school closing down and being left with nothing, so I did the MEP skills test and obtained the licence endorsement as soon as I could after the course. While it wasn't necessary, it gave me peace of mind.

You may ask why I started with the multi-engine instrument rating instead of CPL? To begin your MEIR you only need 70 'pilot in command' hours. I wanted to do my IR on a part-time basis, but instruction was only available to me on Saturdays, so I decided to start with that element first. I would then complete my hour building on Sundays. The CPL requirement, for information, is 100 hours pilot in command and 200 hours total time.

One of the biggest hurdles for anyone wanting to undertake commercial flight training on a part-time basis will be finding a school that offers consistent instruction during the weekend. I was able to find an instructor that was willing to do Saturdays (for IR) and later on, Sundays (for CPL).

With the MEP rating complete (remember, it's up to you whether you undertake the MEP skills test right away or not), I then started my IR training. As I already held the IMC rating and was progressing via the competency-based route, I did not have to do the Basic Instrument Flight Module. The first 30 or so hours of my IR training were spent in the simulator. The course starts gently, drawing 'shapes' in the sky to develop your instrument scan and builds up steadily as your skills improve. The simulator time culminates in flying actual routes with simulated air traffic control. Once the instructor is happy with your standard in the simulator you then move into the real aircraft. IR was probably the toughest phase of flight training for me. Although my IR instructor was fantastic I guess I was just not settled at that specific school. I did not particularly like the flight school management and the booking instability for lessons added to the stress. There was always the constant worry of 'will my lesson be cancelled' which tarnished the experience somewhat. For your IR I would recommend getting a desktop flight simulator to practise what is taught along with 'chair flying'. Chair flying is sitting on your sofa and practising the various aspects of the flight. This can include checklists, rehearsing actions to be taken in an emergency or visualising what you will do during the flight. The more you do to prepare beforehand the more comfortable and smoother the flight will be.

A lot of your success (or failure) on the airfield depends on how you prepare and conduct yourself. The advanced stages of flight training are generally performed to gear the student up to flying in the public transport or airline environment. I would typically arrive an hour before my lesson so I could get a cup of tea and prepare without being rushed. On the odd occasion the instructor would also arrive early, which allowed my lesson to start ahead of schedule and get more out of a given session. The number of students I would see arriving at the flight school 10 minutes before their lesson and not having prepared was staggering. To illustrate, in the airline environment, the first officer prepares the paperwork typically. The airline I work for requires the latest report or checking time forty-five minutes before departure. Suppose you arrive at minute 46 not having prepared or reviewed the various items: weather, route, NOTAMs etc., this is one of the easiest ways to irritate the captain. Sometimes unforeseen events do occur and we are all occasionally late, but don't make a habit of it. Going back to my MEP course I recall during one of the later stages of the course, I had one flight and could not remember the engine failure checks. I ended up having to repeat the lesson because I was concentrating so hard on trying to remember the checks; my capacity for flying suffered. Learn your checks before you go flying!

Most training aircraft are equipped with a glass cockpit or electronic flight instrument systems such as the Garmin G1000. While these offer a high level of capability, you can still make life more comfortable during your training course by learning how to use the systems. There are many online tutorials and feel free to refer to the kcthepilot.com/book page for links to the various apps that I utilised for G1000 training and simulation.

If I had to give tips to the reader on how to pass your IR, I would say the key being open to a flexible plan. It probably will not make much sense now, but IR does have a tendency to be taught in a 'rigid' way with the school predominantly focused on the student passing the IR test. This creates an over-reliance on flying the 'numbers and procedures' without much thought as to what is going on outside the aircraft. A student being trained in this manner tends to be comfortable until the scenario deviates from the rigid instrument rating 'pass your exam only' teaching. Although annoying at the time, what helped me was that my

IR instructor was a bit of a perfectionist. He would not let me move onto the next stage of training until a given exercise was perfect, rather than 'passable'. For this reason, many of those friends of mine undertaking their IR at the same time seemed to be progressing much quicker than me. It was only later I realised that through this excellent work my IR instructor instilled into me the resilience to deal with things that weren't going to plan. For sure my instructor wanted me to pass my IR exam, but he was also focused on making sure I acquired a sufficient depth of knowledge to enable me to cope if the plan changed.

An example of a changing plan was, for reasons outside of my control, I ended up having to fly my IR skills test from an airfield where had not done any training and in a different aircraft (although the same model). There were a few things that came up in my test that were not as 'planned'. I was kept high by air traffic control and then had to fly a non-precision approach asymmetric single-engine when my training so far had suggested that aspect would be flown with both engines running. Another surprise was the examiner requesting that I fly a holding pattern, again, with a simulated engine failure (versus both engines running during training). In hindsight, I probably would not have passed my IR skills test the first time if my instructor had not been so thorough with my training. An instructor with a 'tough' reputation will be better for you in the long run, even if your progress is initially slower. I remember just before my skills test; feedback on my raw data instrument landing system (ILS) was 'passable' but not refined. My instructor insisted I did some remedial work and, while irritating, this extra time at IR stage eventually meant my raw data ILS approaches were robust. I never had any problems during airline assessments when asked to fly these manoeuvres.

The final point to make on the IR is although you will

probably be nervous in the run-up to the skills test – the examiner wants you to pass. If you make a minor mistake, do not worry, keep going. There is some leeway during the test. The important thing is to recognise the divergence and correct it as soon as possible. Provided the infringement was being corrected straight away and safety was not compromised, the examiner will probably let it go and mention it as a minor de-brief item. And oh yes, don't forget to have fun on the IR! The sense of achievement afterwards is fantastic and you do indeed reach an absolute pinnacle of instrument precision flying by the end of your IR training.

Once complete, make sure you request a flight school report and your training records. You will need these when looking for employment. I know I have mentioned this before, but I strongly advise you request your flight school report immediately after your training is complete. Staff in flying schools change frequently and unfortunately flying schools do go out of business from time to time. The last thing you want is to be invited for an airline assessment six months down the road and the interviewing airline request you bring a copy of your flight school report, only for you to find you don't have it and the flying school is no longer trading. The flying school where I did my IR at went out of business four weeks after I completed my skills test.

CHAPTER 10: COMMERCIAL PILOT LICENCE (CPL)

The next stage is to obtain your Commercial Pilot Licence (CPL). This section is quite short as I believe you make or break your CPL experience based on your hour building with most of the items already covered in the hour building section. I ended up doing my CPL Course on a part-time basis with Westair in Blackpool, UK. Money-saving tip: Do your CPL on a single-engine piston aircraft as there's is no need for the CPL to be completed on a twin-engine aircraft. The CPL is aimed at formalising your flying as, during PPL, flying is relatively casual and laid back - for the simple reason that a PPL is for fun and leisure flying. CPL on the other hand, aims to prepare the pilot for public transport flight, i.e. revenue-generating, carrying members of the general public and, more importantly, allows you to earn money from flying.

Crucial to your success during CPL is how you spent your time during hour building. If you were flying around aimlessly going to the same airfields for tea and cake then the CPL tends to be quite challenging. If, however, hour building was full of challenging flights with specific objectives and skills to be practised during each trip, the CPL course is not such a big step.

CPL is all about decision making and captaincy. You will spend a lot of time working on these amongst other things during your CPL course. As CPL students, we joked that everything we did on our CPL course was always wrong. Instructor: "Why are you flying at this level? Why are you using that route? I would not have done it that way." The slightest delay will get you chastised by your instructor. "This is supposed to be public transport flight, HURRY

UP!" The aim is of CPL is always to take the safest, most expeditious route.

The skills test itself is structured similar to your PPL skills test. Still, the expectation in CPL is more formality, precision (tighter tolerances) and complexity (complex aircraft, faster speeds, more airspace, etc.). I followed the items that I described in the hour building chapter (reading the EASA CPL skills test book and maintaining a sharp focus on structured hour building to master the various CPL skills and manoeuvres), and found the CPL course to be very manageable. The PPL to CPL hour building app resource (available at kcthepilot.com/book) provides you with guidance on structured hour building. As discussed in the IR chapter, I recommend you do not take your CPL skills test until you are completely ready and make sure you get a flight school report and your student records on completion.

Suppose I could summarise CPL to the reader, it is a: 'I'm in charge. This is what I am doing, and this is why. If you don't like it, f**k off!' It took me a while to realise, but CPL is a psychological game to get you to grow up with regards your approach to flying.

CHAPTER 11: MULTI CREW COURSE (MCC)

With the CPL and MEIR complete you now have a frozen ATPL. As the focus of this guide is to support your entry into the airline environment; I will not be discussing other avenues for pilot work such as flight instructor, air taxi or surveys flying. With your CPL and MEIR you have the qualifications necessary to pursue these avenues, but I am assuming your goal is employment with an airline and this route requires you to hold a multi-crew qualification.

There are several different types of MCC course. The first type is the bare-bones basic 20-hour MCC course on a generic simulator. These generic devices do not replicate a particular type of aircraft, but are supposed to mirror the approximate performance of a small passenger jet, e.g. hybrid cross between a B737 or A320. These courses typically cost around £2,000. The next type of course is an enhanced MCC which was usually around 36 hours and is conducted on an aircraft-specific fixed training device (i.e. as close as possible replicating a B737 or A320). The enhanced course costs about £7,000. The aircraft specific simulator is reasonably accurate in terms of replicating the aircraft flight deck and handling characteristics. The next type of MCC involves the enhanced MCC, but with the addition of the training company offering to place you with an airline. The enhanced MCC with airline placement can cost around £10,000.

Airlines have been complaining for a long time that 50% or more of candidates who have a CPL & MEIR with an MCC course fail airline assessment. To combat the problem of this high failure rate, EASA created a regulated new type of MCC course called the Airline Pilot Standard (APS) MCC course. The whole idea of this improved MCC is to bridge the gap between CPL/MEIR and airline required skills for employment in a passenger jet that previous MCC courses were not achieving (illustrated by the high failure rate during airline assessment). The APS MCC went deeper into the operation of high-performance swept-wing passenger aircraft, both theoretically and in simulator exercises. 40 hours in the simulator was now the standard for APS MCC. The APS MCC also featured a pass/fail 'test' at the end of the course. The airline assessment pass rate with an APS MCC sits somewhere around 75-85% depending on who you ask.

Rather than try and state which MCC course type is best (as I did not complete all the different kinds of MCC course), I will share my thought process and experience in choosing my MCC course. I started off thinking that the only guaranteed way to secure employment was via one of the MCC courses that provided airline placement (the most expensive type of course). The more people I spoke to, the more I realised that although these schemes offered an airline assessment opportunity, as mentioned earlier, this was no guarantee of obtaining employment. I had heard of pilots who were on these schemes were either stuck in the hold pool or, when finally put forward for placement, the job offers were not suitable (due to e.g. location, terms and conditions, etc.). When there are high levels of recruitment activity amongst the airlines the hold pool (the time it takes for an airline placement) was very short. However, when recruitment slows, hold pool times increased (as long as 12 months plus).

The airline placement schemes came about in the late 2000s as most airlines were only recruiting from the larger schools (with limited exceptions). The larger schools were the main gateway to low hour pilot employment with airlines. Since then and pre-COVID, airlines have been a lot more willing to recruit from outside of these 'established' schools and with the advent of the APS MCC, a lot of doors are now open to low hour pilots. Unfortunately, with the MCC course being the final element of training, most students' budgets have been spent and they are doing their best to finish training with what little is left in the bank. This means most students tend to go for the cheapest MCC course even though the MCC is probably the most crucial part of training as this directly impacts your airline assessment outcome.

To avoid falling into this trap, I suggest you commit to your MCC course early by paying in advance for it. Consider doing a lower cost CPL or IR if money is tight. I often say that if you achieve a mediocre IR (not that I encourage it!), the results can often be salvaged during your MCC course and simulator preparation before your airline assessment. If your MCC course is not up to scratch, the results will be undeniable during your airline assessment. Unfortunately, with airline assessments you only really get one opportunity as, if you are rejected by a given airline, you are barred from re-applying for a minimum of 12 months.

I had also received a lot of feedback that the wait times in these schemes were more than 12 months in the hold pool. For this reason, I didn't think that it made sense to pay a premium for an MCC course on the promise of airline placement only to be sat in a holding pool for months on end. For people who are looking to choose a school or course, please pay particular attention to where their graduates are finding work. I had been looking at VA Airline Training in Cambridge for a while and many of their graduates were successful in landing airline jobs. At the time, although VA did not offer airline placement, many of their students were successfully finding airline employment. Airlines were now giving preference to APC MCC candidates. My goal became to enrol on an APS MCC approved course that I could fit around my annual leave at work. Once there was an APS MCC approved course in the UK, it was an obvious decision to go for an APS MCC course. The decision was an obvious one because some airlines were explicitly stating that APS MCC candidates would be at an advantage during interview and assessment.

I cannot emphasise enough the importance of keeping an eye on what it is you need to do during your flight training to make the transition to an airline job. What are the current trends in airline recruitment? Are particular schools more in favour than others? How long after finishing are people finding jobs? What are those that are securing jobs doing differently to be successful? Speak to as many people as you can in the position you eventually want to be (i.e. recently hired, low hour first officers). This can be at your flying school or via online forums. If going on a flight, at the end of your trip, ask if you can visit the flight deck and chat with the crew. This provided me with lots of encouragement during my training. From the people I spoke to, one of the common themes I found was the relevance the MCC course played on their job outcomes. The people gaining employment tended to have completed the enhanced/APS MCC courses. Although the APS MCC was beneficial in helping secure my first job, one other area that is rarely mentioned is how the MCC course can also help you during your type rating course after securing employment.

The type rating course is the training course that teaches you to fly the specific model of aircraft the airline operates once in employment. I found the APS MCC covered a good 40% of the type rating content for the aircraft I was going to be flying. The APS MCC starts with four days of intensive ground school focused on aircraft systems, performance and standard operating procedures. Although the APS MCC is not meant to be a 'type rating course', the intensity of the preparation and work needed to get through the course means you know what to expect from the type rating. The APS course also structured the simulator sessions in roughly the same way as those on my type rating. During the type rating, we had roughly four consecutive days of 4-hour simulator sessions, followed by four rest days. During the type rating, the idea is that you prepare on your days off for the coming simulator sessions. In a sense, the simulator sessions then become almost a demonstration exercise where you show your instructor that you are proficient in the given tasks. The instructor could then refine and get you to correct any mistakes or address any knowledge gaps. If you approach the sim session expecting to 'learn' from scratch you will find yourself falling behind very quickly as there is nowhere near enough time available. The APS MCC helped me get into the type rating routine (I.e. 4 sims in quick succession followed by preparing for upcoming sims in your own time) and mindset.

It was a tremendous benefit to me that I did my APS MCC course on the same simulator type of aircraft that I would use during my type rating, airline assessment and subsequent employment. I picked an MCC course on the B737 as my main employment targets and indeed the largest employers of low hour pilots in Europe at the time had B737 fleets. My MCC on the B737 was a sizeable head start as I found myself less nervous during the airline assessment and overall, being comfortable with the environment during the interview simulator exercises. The type rating is also relatively straight forward as a result of the APS MCC. Invariably, once the type rating is complete, it is suggested that APS MCC students usually complete their line training in roughly 25% fewer sectors (a single airline flight leg, e.g. a direct flight from Manchester to Berlin would be considered one sector). Line training is the initial period during your airline training process where you initially fly with a training captain. The idea is that the specially qualified training captain aims to improve your proficiency in the real-life, day to day operation of airline flying.

Although the simulator is very realistic, many of the events in the simulator are staged and may not reflect the real-life variability of live airline operations, e.g. air-traffic control delays or interactions with cabin crew etc. I remember when I first started flying operationally for the airline after my type rating; it felt at the time like there was so much going on, particularly in the last 30 minutes or so before pushing back. In the simulator, you don't have interruptions from the cabin crew or the dispatcher coming in and out of the flight deck as you are trying to complete your pre-flight preparation, or the ground crew asking if they can disconnect the ground power as you are in mid-conversation with ATC! Where the APS MCC helps is the additional time you spend in total in the simulator (by the time you start your type rating), you tend to have more capacity for all the 'other jobs' and are further ahead compared to those who have not completed an APS MCC course.

Sales pitch for the APC course over, the final bit of advice I would give for the MCC course (irrespective of which you type of MCC you decide to do) is to request the standard operating procedures from the school and do your best to learn them before the course. Learning the procedures sat in front of a flight deck replica poster (readily available online - ask your MCC school) will make the MCC course much more comfortable and less stressful. In the evenings, after a simulator session, you are mentally fatigued and don't want the added pressure of having to learn standard operations procedures in between simulator sessions. The same would apply for your type rating.

Chapter 12 - Advanced Upset Prevention and Recovery Training (UPRT)

UPRT is a relatively new requirement that all modular or integrated CPL pilots need to complete. The course itself is aimed at training pilots to be able to cope with the physiological and psychological issues of a dynamic aspect in an aircraft. It was introduced following several airline crashes caused by some mishandled aircraft upsets and is one of the improvements to pilot training.

Upset recovery was previously conducted in the simulator, but the new requirement means this training must be completed in an appropriate aircraft. The course itself comprises 5 hours of theory and 3 hours of dual flight instruction from a suitably qualified instructor. The student is exposed to different G situations and upsets; nose high, nose-low (at different bank angles), spiral dives, and stall spin events! The training will develop your competence, resilience and techniques to recover from these very startling situations which, hopefully, the pilot will never see in real life. This section is brief, as the new requirements came in after I completed my training. However, I would encourage the reader to research more via their local CAA and I have included a link to the EASA upset prevention and recovery training 'frequently asked' page via kcthepilot.com/book resource.

CHAPTER 13 - AIRLINE ASSESSMENT

Hopefully, all has gone well during your pilot training and it is now time to get prepared and apply for professional pilot roles. The first step is to prepare your CV. If you have not had a flying CV before there are many examples with guidance on layout etc. online. A simple Google search will provide many results. I did not use any paid service for my CV, but there are plenty of companies out there that offer this facility.

One of the game changers for me in terms of getting the most out of my CV was reading 101 Interview Questions You Will Never Fear Again by James Reed. I highly recommend this book and have shared a link at kcthepilot.com/book. 101 interview questions will help you get behind the psychology of recruitment, help you maximise the impact of your CV and job application and improve your interview technique.

Alongside a current and comprehensive CV your licence and logbook must be in good order, i.e. up to date, ratings valid etc. You will be asked for your passport, licence and copies of the last few pages of your logbook many times over during job hunting. What worked well for me was uploading the key documents onto an online drive so I had the information available quickly whenever needed.

After completing all your necessary information on your job application: name, address, qualifications, licences and ratings, hours, etc., there are the standard questions of 'why you?', 'why this company'? Followed by a series of competency-based questions: What would you do in situation x, y, z? Described a time when you have solved........, etc., etc.

As with any task, practice is the key and, to hone my application and interview skills, I applied for as many jobs as I could, even though many of the companies I applied to were not my primary choice. I acknowledge that, as a low hour pilot, it's tough out there and you may have to take what you are given. However, a sub-optimal opportunity can still be of great benefit in practising for the main target which you may not achieve at the first attempt. Do not waste recruiters time applying for jobs you have no intention of taking though.

Ideally you don't want, for example, your first-ever airline assessment simulator ride to be with the company that you have dreamed of working for since you were a child. The chances are the pressure will get to you and, as a result, you risk performing poorly during the assessment.

Airline applications typically involve some sort of online testing. This tends to be psychometric – reaction speed, verbal and numerical reasoning, spatial awareness etc. Certain external companies offer some practice aptitude tests. I found that some of the exercises were valid, but others are less so. You can prepare for some elements of the aptitude tests, for example, I read a mental arithmetic book to speed up my mental maths.

Many airlines use common platforms for online psychometric testing. This means although you may not have been successful for one opportunity, there are still many lessons to learn that can help you when it comes to psychometric testing in a later assessment. You have probably heard this many times before, but if you get stuck with online testing questions, just move on. I completed one airline assessment where the questions became less difficult as I went along. You may find airline A uses the same company for online testing as airline B. Make all your mistakes with airline A so when you come to airline B's application (your primary target), you are familiar with the setup. You are unlikely to make the same errors again.

Once you get through the first screening stages you will be invited to an assessment centre. Airline assessments typically consist of a technical interview, an HR interview, a group exercise and some type of simulator check. Preparing for an airline assessment takes time, so do not wait until they invite you for assessment before starting your preparation as it will be too late. You may only get a week or, more often than not, a few days' notice for the assessment.

For the technical interview read Ace Technical Pilot (link in the resources) and revisit some of your ATPL notes and the aircraft handbooks (that you have flown) and be familiar with the aircraft types the target company fly.

I will not say much about the HR interview as James Reed's book has that covered. However, what I would add is to read the annual and quarterly reports that your prospective company makes available for investors. It is tedious and yes, financial statements are boring, but annual and quarterly reports can shed a lot of light on the airline. If you are lucky and have multiple job offers, the extra effort you put into understanding the company you are going to work for may one day save you your job. Select companies with robust balance sheets as, over time, they are less likely to go bust and need to make significant headcount corrections. Do not limit your focus on the last few years but read the reports from as far back as is practical. Has the growth been steady? Are they a hire and fire company making drastic corrections in an uptick (lots of recruitment) and lots of redundancies when the business changes? What have the profits and margin been like recently? A company struggling to make money in the good times is going to be at risk in a downturn, as is your job. Indicators of a good airline may include:

- The company has significant cash reserves
- Demonstrates sustained growth in the good times during the last 5+ years (excluding COVID!)
- New aircraft orders in play (even when there is a downturn for whatever reason)
- Good profitability
- Little or no reference to headcount corrections in the last 5+ years (this type of stuff tends to be hidden in the small print towards the back of the report as executives hope no one will read it)

You are being interviewed as the candidate, but this is also your opportunity to talk to your future employer to see if they will be a good fit. My advice is to go with your gut instinct. What is the interview like? Is it rigid and hierarchal? If so, then there is a good chance this culture translates into the flight deck. Can you work with these people?

The assessment may have a group exercise element. Think back to your MCC course and Crew Resource Management (CRM) principles. Try and demonstrate these attributes during the group exercise. The recruiters have no interest in the outcome of the task; they just want to see how you work together. Give other group members a chance to participate, but speak up yourself. If you find someone is unusually quiet, try and bring them into the fold by maybe directing one or two questions at them. Do not dominate the group. The group exercise is an assessment of your CRM. An easy win is designating yourself as a timekeeper at the start of the task. If a decision needs to be made during the group exercise, feel free to suggest using one of the decision-making tools taught during your MCC course like TDODAR (Time, Diagnose, Options, Decide, Assign, Review).

The final aspect of the assessment may include a simulator check where you will be assessed on the 8 ICAO pilot competencies:

- Communication: not just with your sim partner, but with everyone else – ATC, cabin crew, ground crew etc.

- Aircraft flight path management (manual and automatic): the profile varies from airline to airline, but expect a standard instrument departure (SID) or radar vectors, some general handling (climbing, descending, steep turns etc.). Some kind of event leading to recovery/positioning for an approach, typically raw data ILS, but I once had 20kt crosswind visual approach at night instead. The approach generally leads to a low approach to go around, and there may be some asymmetric engine failure work thrown in. The simulator assessment is usually with the experienced flight crew from the airline. They just want to see that you can control the aircraft. They are not looking for perfection. I had a friend on a simulator assessment who managed to stall the aircraft, but they still passed. The crew recognised the mistake, corrected with smooth, coordinated action, and the communication was excellent. On the aircraft flight path management – automation, I was in one airline assessment on an intercept heading for the runway, but the automatics were not set up correctly. My sim partner was a senior captain with the airline I was applying. I mentioned it, and the captain said 'oh sorry, forgot about that' and selected the correct automation we needed immediately. I suspect he was sitting there waiting to see if I would notice and what I would do!

- Leadership and teamwork, problem-solving and decision making: One of the best approaches to your sim check (someone once advised me) was to go into the sim check and do EVERYTHING IN YOUR POWER to help your sim partner pass their assessment. Show the level of initiative and leadership appropriate for the given flying role. If you are pilot monitoring, then allow the pilot flying to take the lead with your input. If you are pilot flying, the assessor will generally be looking for you to lead collaboratively. Use your preferred problem-solving framework, vocalising and using all members of the team – not just your sim partner, but Air Traffic Control (ATC), cabin crew, the company operations team etc.

- Application of procedures: know your sim profile and be a supportive pilot, monitoring if anything is missed.
- Workload management and situational awareness - don't lose sight of the big picture. If you are on fire, don't sit in the hold for 20 mins briefing and doing checklists, get the aircraft on the ground!

Before your assessment, it is worth getting some simulator preparation time booked in to brush up. Look online for the type of sim profile you can expect. There is useful information on the forums (PPRuNe) for this and most sim providers will have an idea of the typical pattern for a given airline. Knowing the pitch and power settings for your aircraft will free up lots of capacity to 'manage the flight'. Hopefully, you get a positive answer a few days later that you passed the assessment!

Other considerations:

There may be a gap from the date you complete your training to landing your first job. During this time, it's a great advantage to be in employment (or have wealthy parents!). Nobody mentions this, but from completion of your training, you probably need in the region of £10k-£15k to keep you going before you earn your first airline salary. Why do you need this money? Well, each interview costs around £1k. You need £500-£600 for a few hours of simulator preparation. You will then need to pay for your accommodation and transport for the airline assessment. That can set you back another £250-£300. If you do not already own a suit, then the budget is blown! Once you have a job offer, most airlines now require a bond or deposit for the type rating. This varies from airline to airline, but it can be in the region of £5k-£10k! The bond is a hedge against the airline losing out financially on its investment in training you and you leaving the company after a short space of time. Once you are on the type rating most airlines will not pay you until completion which takes around three months. For those three months, depending upon your location, you will need to pay for your accommodation and subsistence.

Unfortunately, that's not the end of it. There may be other fees, for example, paying to convert your licence to the national authority of your given airline, security checks etc. It all adds up. It also pays (if you'll forgive the irony) to keep flying if you can afford to do so between completion of your training and getting that first airline job. If you are in employment, all these expenses are much easier to manage. I would even go so far as to say that already being in work took a lot of the pressure off me in terms of having money to live on, being able to meet application costs and not having to accept the first job offer.

Thank you for reading, and I wish you the best of luck in your flight training.

GLOSSARY

AME	Aero Medical Examiner
ATC	Air Traffic Control
BIFM	BIFM – Basic Instrument Flight Module
CAA	Civil Aviation Authority
CBIR	Competency Based Instrument Rating
CRM	Crew Resource Management
DH	Descent Height
DODAR	Diagnosis, Options, Decisions, Assessment, Revision
EASA	European Union Aviation Safety Agency
fATPL	Frozen Air Transport Pilot Licence
FIR	Flight Information Region
ICAO	International Civil Aviation Organisation
IFR	Instrument Flight Rules
ILS	Instrument Landing System

IR	Instrument Rating
IRI	Instrument Rating Instructor
MCC	Multi Crew Course
MDA	Minimum Descent Altitude
MEIR	Multi Engine Instrument Rating
NOTAM	Notice to Airmen
POH	Pilot Operating Handbook
PPL	Private Pilot Licence
SID	Standard Instrument Departure
TDODAR	Time, Diagnose, Options, Decide, Assign, Review
UPRT	Advanced Upset Prevention and Recovery Training
VFR	Visual Flight Rules

Printed in Great Britain
by Amazon